BORN TO BE A BRILLIANT STUDENT :PART-1

--Freedom, dignity and self-worth of a student

AUTHOR

DR.SIBRAM NISONKO, M.A., PH.D

2019

INDIA

TO STUDENTS-A TOCKEN OF LOVE

My dear young friends,

I am eager to write this letter to you probably because this may be one of my last deeds in this life. My last words ,I have decided to dedicate to you since I love you most. Please do not take it as my advice .You are brilliant. You are a gift of the Almighty. You are, therefore, born genius.

Many times I have realized that I can't see what is very close to me due to the mental fact that I ignore what is obvious. I have got a tendency of looking from far and wide for a simple question of life since inquisitiveness is the sign of talent. In this process we follow a common practice of learning by trial and error even though even though the answer is in my hand. Probably your experience is no different than what I have revealed about mine.

2

The message of the book is that students should not try to justify blunders by quoting all the wrongs of history. We have an opportunity to rewrite history by accepting the truth.

Accordingly, my mind has prompted me to undertake this noble project of initiating a straight dialogue with you.

The book is a challenge for a free thought by students. You are given some food for thought on students' frustration and suicide. It then tries to describe the soul of a student, what makes a brilliant students and how to achieve it. There is an additional chapter to solve the problem of unemployment.

Education is the central theme of human development and for centuries it has been believed by wise people that the face of human civilization can be changed by the principles of teaching and learning. Accordingly every society worth a name has its own list of great teachers besides the universal ones like Socrates. We need to search and research the principles that will continue to guide us in our development.

Of course the focus in this book is student because of my thinking that the hand that rocks the cradle is the hand that rules the world.

The book gives a lot of food for thought for all those involved in education. It talks about DIGNITY OF STUDENTS, ACADEMIC FREEDOM, SELF DISCOVERY, SELF -MOTIVATION,

STUDENT COMPETENCIES, QUALITIES OF A
BRILLIANT STUDENT AND MUCH MORE.

I shall be grateful to all of you to let me have your valuable feed
back.

I hope you will enjoy my thoughts and would like to spend some
time on them independently.

Regards,

Sibram, a teacher

INDEX

Chapter -1

THE ANCHORLESS EDUCATION

When the author was young his parents advised him to watch around and see the miracles of events, animals and birds, trees, flowers, moon, sun and stars   around us. But unfortunately he always missed these for a long time due to a shade of dark ring around him. He was fond of childish prank and mischief. On a fine morning he remembered the idea to recollect this poetic thought of his father and realized that a great part of life he had lost due to the meaningless pursuits.

He simply started asking questions. Are we students a meaningless being? Is our birth an accident? Do we all take birth as unwanted? Do we, all human beings, come to earth only to die? Is decay, sufferings and death is the only course of life? Do human lives have no purpose? Are we all helpless cogs in the wheels of creation?

Somebody replied to all these philosophical questions from inside him in a forceful voice: no, no, and no.

During the turn of the century when a child was born the sky was reverberating with the ecstatic melody of the father and mother thus:

Heaven was kind to me

the day they sent me my angel,

Her beautiful little eyes,

her cuddly loving smile

I know so well.

She touched me deeper

Heaven was kind to me

the day they sent me my angel,

Her beautiful little eyes,

her cuddly loving smile

I know so well.

She touched me deeper

than anyone ever did

Flesh of my flesh,

heart of my heart,

a beautiful soul within

When her little arms hug me

I feel empowered to go on.

By Clive Williams

(A Real Angel)

We need to reflect at this time where we have lost our vision. Let our children grow as fearless beings ,without guilt or shame and speaking nothing but the truth. They move on earth like air, water or sunshine.

Beauty and the beast

Today's man has become rich and wise while children have become sad. Children have lost so many precious things, one of which is their innocence . Today's child finds his life shattered every minute due to unsettled life of parents, unprincipled teachers and the heartless deadwood peers.

Ill fares the land, to hastening ills a prey, Where wealth accumulates, and men decay:

By Oliver Goldsmith
(The Deserted Village)

Unwanted changes kill   the humanity

As the society and country are growing smaller and smaller due to globalization effect ,aspirations of new generation people are soaring with lightening speed causing unimaginable strain on child psychology. Because of historical reasons more than 20 % children come from poor families. Many from these children, no doubt, rise to the highest level given opportunities. But the emerging political situation has energized them to jump the steps. They want quick results. Since there is mismatch between ability and expectations depression and tension set in leading to violent reactions.

Centuries together education has remained to be a hand maid of ruling class whose main aim is to have over riding control over money, men and the wealth of the country. Due to recent social changes a new class has emerged whose primary aim is to copy the western culture so that they can compete with the elite ruling class. There came a time of resurgent political society with it a rise of middle and lower classes who want to out-sign the traditional rich people by acquiring modern skills. But the skills the modern education has given to them are nothing but short cuts to accumulate money and a little power and position in the society. The whole system of education has drained away men from human values and ethical practices. It has made educated men selfish, mean and arrogant both inside and outside.

The situational variance describes a complex situation in the educational field .It requires a thorough reversal of our vision about parental responsibilities, educational reforms, teacher development and positive school administration.

Before a child celebrates his second birthday, she is thrown into the hands of a strange ayah who is just opposite to her mother. She faces all the challenges of a strange behavior, awkward culture, unknown language, unfamiliar food and peculiar dress and make up. Very quickly the child is forced to kill her innocence. She can neither cry nor tolerate. Same is the story of a child who is sent to nursery school.

Today's parents have lost their path in the cement jungle and force their daughters to grow fast as the Queen of England or Rani Jhansi and sons to be the Alexander the great or the Prince of Monaco or Albert Einstein.

The vested interests

In developing countries which have recently freed from the clutched of foreign rulers, we see emergence of a neo-elite hypocritical group, They are educated in private convent schools, sometimes abroad, running their own business or employed in white color high profile jobs. They loiter with expensive smart phones, having little idea GDP or per capita income or inflation affect on the life of a common man. They are not inclined to support any progressive project to benefit the large number of under-privileged public.

They blame the government for welfare measures meant for masses. Ironically they criticize the government for the inadequacies in public service like transport or banking just because they don't get the priority. They hate to participate in public service improvement programs. Education is a victim of such privileged people who have the power to manage the policy of the government and the administration with ease.

They are born to enjoy all that is good in this world. They want to enjoy all alone everything that come on their way. Through their

12

power, position and wealth these so called national development promoters perpetuate corruption, inefficiency, anti-social and anti-national activities causing a wholesale destruction of precious human resources. In this situation more crimes are carried by so-called educated charlatans than any identified criminal. Facts speak louder than this voice.

It is a fancy for them to use celebrated words such as freedom .intolerance, secularism, constitution, fair treatment, justice in public domain , meaning that the country is obliged to provide these benefits exclusively to them. To them morality and ethics are middle class malaise.

They pay Taxes, considering it to be their charity to the country's poor. With ancestral riches they could make their children IAS officers or MBBS doctors. They take pride in throwing insulting comments on our country and eager to migrate to a developed country as NRIs. They live an exclusive life of new generation elite.

Education in the country is suffocated in the hands of such elites who show little seriousness on such issues as human rights of children, their education, life of deprived children, infrastructure for their primary education or their development .Even though a radical change is imperative, such change is possible when a large number of people from the affected mass will become aware of these issues

.Their awakening will lead to fruitful action ending at core transformation.

The needs of the hour are growth oriented philosophy of education, implementation of values, designing of pro-active programs and providing a meaningful life through right education to a large number of children of common men who have been deprived of the same since ages.

Missing parents

Everybody feels excited to be a parent but nobody wants children. A great practical joke! Delivery of premature child, scissoring delivery, IV treatment for childless parents, surrogacy, adoption of children nursery school and many such choices are invented by men and women to satisfy their urge for children. At the same time there is a huge demand for baby sitters, ayahs to look after children, girls hostel, boys hostel, paying guest hostels for students, mess for students and many such facilities are ample evidence that we don't like to take the direct responsibility of nurturing a growing child. Many don't like to share the pleasures and pains of growth of their children. Children generally become victims in rich society as parents bother more about their status, position and reputation than their children education.

To add fuel to the fire the UNICEF has found that a large number of children become victims of domestic violence in every year. Defenseless children face innumerable violence ranging from physical injury, psychological abuse, negligent treatment, exploitation to sexual abuse. The perpetrators may include parents and other close family members.

A small survey of educational practices in schools both in urban and rural areas leave us in distress. The data, views and experiences of those who matter in education reveal that there is everything else in our schools except education. Learning has left schools.

School or a commercial centre

Because the promoters of private schools consider students as customers, they don't hesitate to exploit them finically by offering multiple co- curricular activities and fanciful subjects. They provide summer camps, facilities of holiday resorts.

School or a community service centre

Many schools use students as social workers for cleaning roads, working as traffic police, serving beggars etc. Although these activities may by themselves are appreciable they don't add up to the goal of learning. Let us reduce the school time for freeing them for other social skills.

School or a laboratory for nascent politicians

After the author passed his 11th standard he joined a junior college for further studies. Within the next three months of joining he found a group of good –for- nothing students picketing at the gate to prevent students from going to class, under the influence of the local charlatans. When the author approached their petty leader to find the reason for the strike, their simple reply was that they wanted to form a college union of students to guide the College Administrators.

The author protested telling that their studies were disturbed. His simple reply was that all their problems would be solved after he became the President of the college union. Strange! Every second man joins an educational institution today prepares for a political career. May be because it does not require any brain; It gives any Tom-Dick- and Harry an unlimited power, position and wealth without efforts.

School or ornament shop

I have friends having triple degrees like M.A.(History),M.A.(Political Science), and LL.B still seeking a white color job without success. They are just waiting for Good Samaritan or a politician to support them .Till such time they rely on the wisdom of their old parents. They can neither tighten a screw on the bathroom tape nor can they write an official memo in sales job. They seem to be using these degrees to cover up their nakedness.

The deserted island

There is another land called rural India. More than half of them are below 25 years. They need employment. They observe that the major chunk of job opportunities are pocked by the English speaking urban mass and they presume that the latter's English education along with multi-skilled education provides them the advantage of modern schools run by private operators. These operators have nothing in their mind except making profit out of the ignorance of their customers. They don't seem to have a standardized educational practice. Their teachers are ill trained to nurture the talents from the villages.

In the name of modernization we tend to have more trained stone cutters with good kills than trained teachers with good skills to take care of integrated needs of a student .We prefer to have more gold testers than educational counselors.

The Pandora's box

In a modern school there are wise policy makers, highly qualified administrators and very highly energetic teachers. Their contribution to the organization called "school" can't be measured since such schools never existed in the past. They have introduced every big thing under the sky to shakeup a student and even the parents. The list of activities runs into pages and there is stiff competition between the players. What is their impact on real learning?

Loss of self- motivation

Most problems with motivation come from subconscious thought patterns. Interestingly, many of these patterns are *intended* to motivate you. The difficulties with these thought patterns are that they are ineffective strategies learned long ago when you had no idea what was going on.

Other causes of poor motivation come from subconscious mind. Students get attached to self-deprivation early in life That continues as a habit .They don't try again to lead a better life. They develop a self-killing motivational pattern that works like slow poisoning.

Psychological disability

Freedom and dignity of children are nipped at the bud first by the ignorant parents and later by the selfish, greedy school teachers.

Over ambitious parents and unethical teachers kill innocence of children. They force the young mind to be non-motivators. Their initiative is killed. With fall in self-motivation children develop a series of negative psychological tendencies like:

1. Disrespect to self.
2. Helplessness
3. Flattering and pleasing negative characters
4. Procrastinating and postponing
5. Deprivation attachment

6. Easy contentment

7. Stoicism.

8. Loner feeling

9. Confused

10. Empty mindedness

11. Dependence on artificial support system like use of toys to fill up the time and obtain thrill and excitement to fill emptiness.

Chapter-2

STUDENTS, REGAIN YOUR DIGNITY

"If we are to teach real peace

in this world,

and if we are to carry on

a real war

against war,

we shall have to begin

with the children"

---Mahatma Gandhi.

Look at your soul

You are the real messengers of peace. When a child feels peace in mind he spreads his air of peace in family, society, organization he lives in and the universe as a whole.

Your soul is your faith on self. You need to be self directed, a torch-bearer and be beacon light unto yourself, although you may seek help from significant others like teachers, family members and peers. You grow strong when you have a strong reference group. You start respecting the elders in your family since they have experience .You respect your teachers since they have skills to teach, knowledge and insight. You love your peers since they can encourage you and provide you emotional supports. When strong roots are ensured the tree can grow by itself.

With power of self you can spread all around, friendliness, positive feelings; you will be active to keep the surrounding clean and bright and you will never feel frustrated in doing so. You will come out of meanness and emptiness. You will be able to nourish those who fail to support themselves. You will always try to acquire good human qualities from all sides so that you will grow into one who can be a savior instead of dependent on others. That way you will be a source of inspiration for those who will follow your footsteps.

Power of self comes from the power of your faith on the creator. Remember that the creator has created you in his image. A natural child is spontaneous, willing, free, fearless, spirited and confident. What can be said of a positive social atmosphere! A child, in free air ,develops loving, devotional, affectionate, compassionate, hopeful, cheerful, optimistic, comfortable, warm, pleasant and enjoying qualities. With experience of kind , clean ,pure ,lively ,agreeable and peaceful physical and human environment the inherent qualities of openness,autonomy,insight,relaxation,friendliness,.righteousness,ho nesty,determination, stable decisiveness, fixed, closeness , vigor ,powerfulness flourish within the mind of a child.

See the beauty of life

There is beauty in the eyes of your mother, father, brother and sister because beauty actually does not appear on eyes but is found in their heart. You must be able to look at their heart to appreciate their beauty. Similarly there is beauty in the heart and mind of your teachers. It is reflected in their love for you, their commitment towards your learning and their dedication to the school..Your real world is constituted by dozens of such selfless people. Don't ever forget or neglect their contributions.

All the earliest saints and philosophers have arisen from the most depressed conditions. They inspire you to arise and awake, and success will be in your hand. Everything rests on you in life. Fulfillment of life is the product of faith on your own self. Faith leads to action that breeds results. Good faith manages   good emotions.

An equation can be formulated thus:

$$SS = f(F.E.A)$$

Where SS=student's success

f=function of

F=faith of students

E=emotions of students

A=actions that are positive

Self directed students

Let you grow as self-directed student, rather than work-for rewards, avoiding punishment or for your own learning. Bad results have reasons. They are not due to luck but because of laziness or negligence. You don't go by the idea that teachers are unfair to you. With adequate motivation and commitment, in the long run, you will get the rewards and recognition you deserve. Your efforts will be reduced when you think that your grades in the school are influenced by many accidental happenings. As good student you need to work sincerely and at the same time use opportunities available to achieve your career goal. You must extend cooperation and seek cooperation when needed. You can influence people and win them to like you. Art of friendship can be learned if required. A well prepared student does not blame the examiner or the question paper. He is comfortable in all situations. Conflicts can be avoided if you go with positive mind, whether in family in friends group. Although life is not simple always and we have to face complex situations

25

sometimes, you can pass through the hurdles smoothly with positive thinking, right preparations. It does not direct you to go against God; rather it wants you to live with hope and faith in god's world. You should feel responsible for the outcome of your efforts, instead of blaming on parents, teachers, and school or education system. You will get all that you deserve when you strengthen yourself.

Competencies of students

A competent student has realistic perception about himself and the world around him. He takes initiative to search outside solutions for problems instead of easily admitting failure. He is motivated by a sense of personal responsibility. While obey the social rules they are also spontaneous, open and unconventional.

Try to be a systematic being. That is the beginning of a student life. Develop a mental picture about your strengths and weaknesses. Develop an overall feeling of your personal worth and value since you have ability to perform with right thinking and self regulation. Remember that you have ability to bounce back and recover from failure at any time.

There are many saints and many views. Listen to all but act what convinces you. You can't be perfect just by listening to all and changing and again changing your plans now and then. Listening to different views may help you to check your facts and your reality. Young minds are victims of high sounding suggestions. But

26

remember that all changes are not desirable. Changes should be based on confirmed values and facts. Listen, think and act.

Don't justify your blunders by quoting all the wrongs of history. You have an opportunity to rewrite history when you confront with the truth. The return journey starts from you.

Rationalizing past blunders is a serious negative attitude. It will continue to make us take foolish actions and continue doing blunders. We will never be able come out of such a vicious circle. We will be going farer and farer from truth and a precious opportunity to improve is lost, although one may relax being free from taking responsibilities. Wise man learns from his mistakes and progresses by listening to feedback and even criticisms.

Respect your self

When you respect yourself you set achievable goal and work actively for its achievement. You don't keep your tasks pending. Delaying or postponing an important task like preparing for an examination till an emergency situation is faced makes you panic and then you shout at yourself or punish yourself .It further hurts you .The cycle continues till some of you develop a dangerous impulse like committing suicide.

Feel assured, capable and strong.

It starts with first response to a hurdle. You stop and then take a shortcut or immediately run for help. With that practice a habit id developed and when the source is not available you become helpless. That is a negative habit. As you take the first step, the road will be clear.

Balance your needs with the needs of others.

As a social being we are all interdependent. You may sometimes feel like going out of the way to please others so that you may gain some favor out of the way. It is selfishness and makes you yield for satisfying others mean needs. Logically you adjust your needs according to your strengths and to the extents they don't come on other's way.

Be practical

It is said that nobody can be greater than his boots since without good condition boots you can't work efficiently. You need to accept the daily drudgeries of cleaning, washing and account keeping. When you neglect the initially they accumulate to spoil your sleep. You work on these things by thinking of their final results and comforts that they will give at the end.

Source of happiness within you

Nobody is perfect and nothing can make you perfect. Motivation makes you more motivated. Experience every small achievement and enjoy. Concentrate on your present. Love your work. By accepting failure quickly you conclude that deprivation is your way of life. Change in your present situation to a great extent lies in your hand.

Have a little ambition

Low ambition people have low motivations. Dreams and ambitions are everybody's birth right. Why should you deny them yourself? When you are resourceful you will automatically raise your ambitions. Ambitions should match with the reality, your capabilities and resources.

Poverty, lack of education and extreme environmental conditions make people stoic. They learn to get pleasure out of deprived conditions. Education depends upon personal desires. External conditions can be changed. With these two measures it will take little time to fight against poverty.

Be a team man.

 As a social being we need to stay connected with people .We need to be communicative to maintain relations. Social media, although helps in re-establishing lost relations, destroys our contacts with near ones when it reaches the level of addiction. Maintaining quality time with present relations and friends is essential for our socio-psychological health.

Work on your goals

We lead a confused life when our goals are not clear. Work on your goals step by step taking facts in to consideration without being impulsive. Think before you act since that will change the course of your life. Unfortunately, many students just follow some off-hand suggestions of old family friends, neighbors or parents without fully analyzing the implications.

Be on the present

With innumerable forces acting on one mind mindfulness becomes difficult for a student. It leads to empty mindedness. One needs to delink attention from those unwanted forces and suggestions. By focusing on present issues solutions can be found and learning can be improved. To adjust with unrealistic situation created by forced goals, unclear subject and unfriendly climate students develop absent mindedness and take resort to artificial support system like playing with doles, drinks and drugs. The solution to this lies in being practical.

You need to urgently set yourself free by learning about the ineffective motivation patterns that hold you back. Retain the enthusiasm of a child since the child is your real self. The child in you enjoys the beauty of Nature in its original form. He experiences a sense of ecstasy, enchant and joy with the natural phenomenon. He remains closer to the spirit of Divinity. Nothing that does not preserve these invaluable qualities of the child is worth pursuing in the name of education.

Develop self-confidence

"Once we believe in ourselves,

we can risk curiosity, wonder,

spontaneous delight, or

any experience

that reveals the human spirit."

– E.E. Cummings

Student life is an exciting period of one's life. You have unlimited possibilities of growth with plenty of opportunities, resources and a large number of well wishers around. Nothing should stop you having a great sense of self-worth , a feeling of joy in life and in activities, freedom from self-doubt, freedom from fear and anxiety, freedom from social anxiety, and stress. You must feel full of energy and motivation to act. You must enjoy interacting with other people at social gatherings. You feel relaxed and make others in your company feel relaxed.

Concentrate on success stories

You start with positive efforts to make improvements in life. Always think about your good qualities and be conscious of your mental and physical well being.

 While in family group, school or play ground behave as equal and maintain good relationship with class mates and siblings.

It is very significant that you feel satisfied with yourself and feel happy in whatever work you do. You show your willingness and enthusiasm while you have to work in groups and take initiatives to get good results .Break your goal into smaller activities and achieve them and that way proceed step by step to gain self confidence. Keep your body relaxed and open while talking to others. Keep yourself physically fit and energetic and keep growing every day. Trust your own abilities, capacities, and judgments, or belief that you can successfully face day to day challenges and demands. You can be in a success track when your memory concentrates on what you have achieved so far and your past success experiences not misses and failures.

Chapter-3

WHAT MAKES A STUDENT BRILLIANT

Self discovery

When you grow you start knowing yourself. That will make you empowered .You feel victorious and emit rays of hope and abundance. You feel free to make a choice in education, career style of life or physical well being. You give full attention to your dreams, passions and wishes.

Character

Character is formed by simple life, plain food, good conduct. It means simple living and high thinking. Character is a comprehensive term comprising of faith, trust, empathy, courage, fortitude, honesty, loyalty and good behavior..When you start good habits character will automatically be built. The most important element of character is

35

your faith on goodness of life and the good intention of the creator who created you. Trust on established values, be empathetic to your neighbors, have courage to do the right things, be honest and sincere in dealings with people, be loyal to your institution and show good conduct. That is how you can uncover the most mysterious enigma called character.

Faith on God

Faith on self is faith on God and faith on positivity. As you grow you develop a set of beliefs, convictions, natural feelings or acceptance. All civilized people , all over the world have expressed their faith on God, religion, spiritual teachers , Scriptures and Teachings of Saints because it is believed that faith on the qualities of god help human beings to develop the qualities that help society to flourish.. They are responsible for your identity and morality. These beliefs influence your thinking and behavior. These are the inner sources that help you to overcome doubts and uncertainties in life. It stabilizes your mind. Faith on God helps you to be organized. Faith develops purity of body, mind and knowledge. You develop faith when your parents also support you.

You and your parents need to get the support from scriptures, spiritual teachers and saints. Faith in God leads to faith in every individual soul. Faith in humanity necessitates faith in Nature because survival of mankind is impossible without the blessings of the Nature, the environment .Thus the journey of faith pulls us to have faith on the society and the great personalities that have shaped our civilization and culture.

With noble faith human beings surrender to the higher needs of society, selflessness and sacrifice while demonic faith develops in men qualities of greediness, selfishness, cruelty and violence. It helps you to be devotional, reasonable, obedient, kind and compassionate. You like to be bound to regulations, discipline and systems and procedures. They encourage sincerity in faith which in turn makes them sincere in their actions and intentions. With sincerity of faith students can achieve worldly goals honestly. They will pursue justice and fair-play when grown up. All modern illness among children comes from our inferior faith. We live in ignorance and delusion in the name of modernity and advancement.

You will get more of what you focus in life. If you focus on problems, you live solely in those problems and have difficulty moving past the negativity. Therefore you focus on positivity and seek out solutions so that you can resolve your problems and move from a state of poverty back to a state of richness. Train your mind to do so ,since it doesn't happen automatically. For a little time things may not be in your favor. Continue in the right path so that it will take no time for change to take place.

Faith is strength

Faith on good things will show you right path. Trials and tribulations are the way of life. Faith will guide you and you can proceed towards your purpose of life during trouble time while overcoming stress, anxiety and fear. Without faith things will start deteriorating. You will develop mental anguish along with physical sickness.

Faith on life

Faith on god means faith on life since it is god's creation, not human creation. God has made all of us to thrive and survive. There are problems to days indicating that better things are going to come tomorrow. Living today is a strong reason to achieve something tomorrow. For every hurdle think and search you can find an answer. It may take a little time

Continuity of learning

Learning is an integral part of human life. Every experience and every stage of life give us opportunities to learn. Learning helps us in thinking right and gaining knowledge. Inner abilities, attitude to learn and practice and intuitions   play greater role in your learning though money, technology and infrastructure, books, discussions are facilitators of learning.

Your past experience and knowledge is your personal wealth. Use them effectively. Focus on collaborative relationships between yourself, parents and schools to support the continuity of learning and transitions.

Self –reinforcement

Self –reinforcement means setting your own goal, however insignificant,   monitoring and evaluating own performance and self-feedback. As a self-regulatory mechanism it plays a more prominent role than external reinforcement   in learning process. It is an easy way to regulate your behavior and motivation. You can strengthen your learning by rewarding yourself with feeling of happiness, sharing your knowledge with one who wants it and by acquiring new skills.

Joy of learning

Good learning is inherently pleasurable.

Self-acquired values, knowledge, and skills are energizers that invigorate a child's mind toward an uncharted land of imagination. Each step of success in this path generates a sense unique pleasure for him.

If you destroy the pleasure of learning   you are also destroying the pleasure of living. A healthy individual can grow like   a healthy tree under   favorable conditions. A human child needs conducive social conditions   to grow with good physical health as well as psychological health. It is the responsibility of the parents, peers and the school system to develop the child as a brilliant student. Always it should remind the child that he has a unique   privilege of getting educated and be successful in life. Before we talk about education and role of students or teachers let us examine the philosophy of education and its purpose, the direction and the speedometer of education.

Chapter -4

HOW A STUDENT BECOMES BRILLIANT

The essentials to learn

Human beings have come from stars and will return to stars after a
short earthly tenure. During this period we need to work our best that
is assigned to us. As a student my sole responsibility is to learn.
While learning we have to be a normal person, neither too harsh nor

too soft on physical ground . The process of maturity for a normal person is education.

Mugging up of a large body of information can't be education. It is only a routine of a beast of burden.

The essentials to learn for children are those that are relevant to their personal life as well as to their social life. They should acquire knowledge that will fetch them job and make them fit to serve the country. Since we are a young nation our children should be able to lead the country in future. Accordingly we need to learn the science and commerce subject to become Industrialists and scientists. This is possible when we learn with awareness of the philosophy behind a subject, and reason behind a phenomenon. Since we are the makers of a new Society our children should not lack in moral and social competency.

Citizenship

A bare minimum that a student has to learn in school is citizenship since it is the Nation that gives security to our life and property. It is the responsibility to learn and be able to differentiate between what is right and what is wrong, what is immoral and what is moral &

what is just and what is unjust, the power to question anything wrong, learn the right way to achieve what are desirable for you and behave positively, find the truth and feel free to think in different social aspects and remove ill beliefs. An excellent student is one who is aware and confident; who has ability to grow into a capable citizen.

The goal of education is also to form children into human persons committed to work for the creation of human communities of love, fellowship, freedom, justice and harmony. Students are to be molded only by making them experience the significance of these values in the process of education.

As a student you learn to live as equals, participate in all jobs of housekeeping and keep the residence livable in and around the school and the hostel.

Scientific temper

You should develop scientific temper so that you decisions become objective; you develop spirit of inquiry and get new answers to old sticky problems.

Technological skills

Innumerable technological innovations are being developed everyday in our environment about which a learner can't remain oblivious. Students can improve their performance by developing the essential skills in technology as these skills will make them efficient .It will reduce monotony and save time.

Human nature is multisided with multiple needs, which are related to life, all aims are correlated to ideals of life,

The goal of education is to be the full flowering of the human on this earth, According to UNESCO the physical, intellectual, emotional and ethical integration of the individual into a complete man/woman is the fundamental aim of education.

Liberty, equality and fraternity are the essential qualities of a human community. A student has to learn these values of community living and show commitment to these values. A school is the richest place to be able to share and inculcate these values among the students.

Teachers could achieve this only by the living example of their lives manifested in hundreds of small and big transactions with students in word and deed. A teacher is neither a power centre nor a man of unlimited riches. His simplicity is an education in action for his followers.

As an educated person one hopes to solve the problems humanity faces today.

Being Useful to the society

Survival and growth of this little world of human beings is possible only when we learn to live in peace and harmony with each other and defend ourselves together from the enemies. In a harmonious society, there is no place for negative emotions like lust, aggression. They cause threat to others. You discipline your mind by reasoning and following established procedures. Follow the principles of cooperation early in life so that you can acquire a vision of cohesive society of which you can be a founder.

We live in an entangled society where all of us are dependent on each other for various types of day to day requirements. Skills development on such commonly demanded tasks will make us easily employable. With such common skills one can get jobs on hourly and daily basis. It can help us easily balance the demands of service as well as that of family.

"Every child is born a genius."

-Albert Einstein

It requires freedom for a child to express himself, to develop his potentialities. The power of a developed society with full of wisdom and achievements pales into insignificance unless we can provide this little care that our little child needs. Every child is different and that directs us to treat him differently so that all our affords and activities end in the child's development.

A child is curious and creative by birth. It is the mother who can find sense of the information that she gets from the child. With this knowledge parents may start the process of empowerment and build the child's confidence. What counts at this stage is to meet the child's hunger for knowledge and understanding and create an environment help him to apply with creativity and objectivity. One can't acquire happiness or prosperity with the blindness and ignorance that pass though either at home. When a child grows in an atmosphere of nuclear family , contract marriage, single mother family or pre-schools, nursery schools, distance education, on-line education ,part-time education, these goals of learning is a far cry.

This change in children is evolutionary not revolutionary. Every day is a learning time for a child. He can't learn everything as a capsule in a compressed time frame. Making him independent, making him aware of bad and good things of the world will make him grow. Sometimes children get the blame that they are naughty. It is a misunderstanding of his demand for a different approach to his needs .He needs more attention and support. He asks ,a teacher to get closer to him, listen to him and work with him for his learning needs.

Link learning with life goal

Learning becomes real and exciting when it is linked with one's own passion .Education and employment are closely linked. It provides opportunities to contribute in community services by linking personal requirements with community opportunities.

Merit or potential of a child is universal but absence of appropriate place or environment can prove a child meritless. Anybody can earn his rewards with right preparations. A minimum that any educational activity can contribute is to make the student fit for a job and earn his economic self-sufficiency. Nobody's merit can be denied for this minimum achievement. There is a major difference between being a degree holder and an educated man. We need a student to achieve more than a degree to be a doctor or engineer, scientist or astronaut, leader or professor. A work is this direction is counted to be worthy only if it can make a difference in the personal life of child when he grows as a man. The finest ideal of the goal of education is to live and enjoy more beauty and more happiness. In absence of this the very purpose of civilization is lost. Alcohol is obnoxious to health and still people drink it irrespective of their needs. An educated person gives it up once he knows it while a certificate holder will still continue drinking. A mere certificate in education is not worth the paper.

My hope of the future lies

in the youths of

character, intelligent,

renouncing

all for the services of

others, and obedient

– good to themselves and

the country at large.

-

Vivekananda

You need to grow into youths with nerves of steel, an impressive
ability to remain calm in dangerous or difficult situations,, muscles
of iron with full of strength and bravery and minds like
thunderbolt having compassion and wisdom that can forthwith

eliminate ignorance, greed and cruelty. Your mind should be intensely eager to get the answer to problems that come to you.

Find music in life

Sweet words and expressions between family members, peers in the education institutions and between students and teachers are like music in life. Students as a big group should never forget this reality. With positive feelings towards each other your mind generates capability to be creative. It will also develop capabilities of imagination and liveliness.

Positive emotions

Students have to face high level of pressures during their learning period which might trigger various range of emotional experiences. Many times it has been observed that anxiety, anger ,envy , freight , sadness ,shame , jealousy and dissatisfaction generate further stress facilitate adaptation leading to low performance while positive emotions like hope, and success are intimately related. It is for psychological benefits you need to select consciously certain fundamental positive emotions for greater learning ahead,

GRATITUDE

51

You have been receiving limitless possessions, facilities and attention of many people. You need to be grateful to people who ensure these things for you.

HOPE

You have been receiving things of your need and liking from birth. So you need to feel hopeful that these things will continue to be given to you in future also.

AWE

The love and dedication of your mother, father, friends and relatives and your teachers –all these are grand, overwhelming and unearthly. In fact ,the entire world around you is spectacular. All these should provide you the necessary sense of awe for the whole life.

KINDNESS

You must have seen plants, clouds, the sun, air and earth. They all are very selfless and generous in serving the human kind. Let every one of you learn these qualities and show some kindness to others.

CONTENTMENT

Every time you get something in this world of scarcity you must feel contented as you can see how millions live in deprivation.

CONFIDENCE

There are beautiful animals living in ocean, on earth, on trees and in caves without fear. Why should you as human beings, with so much of resources, not live with confidence?

ADMIRATION

We need to warmly approve, appreciate and respect those who do many good works for you, day in and day out. It is natural to appreciate them.

EAGERNESS

You have to show readiness and excitement for doing any desirable thing in life. This will give you more energy to perform better.

Social intelligence

Give attention to and show respect, to all category of people in the school like teachers, guides clerks, gardeners and security staff.

Your interest in them will be reciprocated by them for your long-term growth and development. Take initiative to build good relations. Listen to the ideas of friends and class mates with a purpose to develop a mutual supporting relationship   . Understand others difficulties as a normal practice and in that process enjoy helping and contributing to the happiness of other people.

How to seek help from teachers

Whenever possible try to figure out the solution to your problem on your own before you ask your teacher for help. When this is a common problem by many others and you really can't solve for yourself., in this situation seeking help is a mature thing. Get your teacher's attention the right way. , like raising hand or saying "excuse me" etc..Tell your teacher what you need help with. You may be a little specific in explaining your difficulties.
Don't ask your teacher for the answers. .Instead, ask how you can find the answer. With respect to the teacher and with attention listen to the response

How to seek help from parents

There is nothing wrong in seeking help from parents. Students can't be expected to be perfect. Small omissions and commissions are opportunities for learning. Students also should not feel ashamed of minor mistakes. Instead, it is always advisable to seek help from parents in such cases. Select suitable moment. Explain the problem and your feeling about the whole thing. Say clearly that you want their help.

How to seek help from peers

Luck ,destiny and god don't help you directly, but your peers can. So seek their help when desirable. Don't delay it thinking ,it does not matter or it will not make any difference.

Sometimes your feeling of powerlessness may stop seeking help. When your beliefs don't match with your actions, you become inactive. Open your eyes and reach out.

How to seek help from family members

Sharing appreciations among family members is the best way develop relationship and strengthen your emotional personality. Developing family support system

You can seek help from your family at a desirable time provided there is attempt has already been made to develop family support system like relying on each other to fulfill one's responsibility without pressure, problem solving abilities are learnt step by step from the childhood, You should actively participate in family meals, family functions, family prayers, family entertainment and family sports.

1. **Be open and Honest**

   By being open and honest you can start with a positive foundation to build your relationship with friends.

2. **Mutual Respect**

   Listen and respect the ideas ,thoughts and opinions of friends so that you can work together, find solutions to common problems. Respect their wisdom, insight and creativity

3. **Emotional balance**

   Be careful about what you say and what you don't with special attention to words, emotions and gestures. Balanced emotions are essential even for managing emotions of others.

4. **Be positive**

   Accept diversity of people and listen to their opinions. Take time to consider what they have to say use their insight for your decision making.

5. **Be communicative**

   Use all opportunities to be in touch with your friends. Friendship, love and companions are divinely bestowed on man only: Other worldly creatures are deprived of it. Be in touch with your social contacts.

6. **Schedule time to build relationships**.

    Give time to your friends and class mates since they are an integral part of your life.

7. **Appreciate others.**

   Since everybody is endowed with many good human qualities it is a precondition for developing a relationship with anybody to identify and appreciate those qualities. Speak positively about your friends and class mates in their presence and more so in their absence.

8. Manage your boundaries.

It is not a quality of a wise man to have opinion on every topic and comment on what others say. Sometimes silence is golden. One should know when to react and how on subjects that may affect him. If our opinion will have negative impact on others' behavior it is better to reserve one's opinion.

9. Avoid gossiping.

Gossiping about others in their absence is bad in relationship building.. Similarly one should avoid gossiping on matters related to others and they are not related to us.

10. Share more of you at welcome meeting

In a friends' circle or in peer meetings sharing information about us will help us make new friends and bring us closer to our old friends.

11. Volunteer to help others in their need

People like friend who voluntarily comes forward to extend his helping hand . It is important to be liked by others since modern life is mostly complex and we all are interdependent in our daily life.

12. Write thank you notes

It is a sign of an educated person to express our "thanks "for whatever help we receive in normal life. It may be done either orally or better in writing..

13. Initiate conversations by asking questions

Art of conversation is an essential quality of making friends. Asking simple questions may help people to divert their attention towards you.

14. Participate in Group work

Participate in activities other than class work, like picnic, group worship, book exhibitions, sports and games

Trust your   parents

1. Use polite language in your talks with them. .In this world of dog eat dog who else can be more concerned about you than your parents.. They are selfless and are eager to help and support you. Always be modest and allow them to finish their talk since they have long years of experience and their experiences may be rich with wisdom..These are simple principles of showing respect to your parents

2. While interacting with your parents, keep calm .Do not seek their opinion unless you are willing to listen.

3. Be positive and warm in your body language.

4. Be open and honest while talking to your parents.

5. When you are grown up avoid unnecessary arguments and avoid topics where you think you have basic differences.

Master learning skills

Students learn in different ways – some learn by seeing, some by hearing, some by reading and some by doing. This is the reason for you to take time at early age to play with other children as it is a great way for you to develop the skills you need to get on with others. Your community connections can offer valuable learning experiences too.

The modern proven methods of learning skills are critical thinking, creative thinking, communicating, and collaborating.
These skills help you learn with ease, and so they are vital to succeed in school and beyond.

Etiquettes and manners

A man is known by his culture comprising of one's language of expression in social interaction, the unwritten rules that one follows. Manners and etiquettes fall under this category.

Manners and etiquettes are elements of culture, the rules and the guidelines which specify the behavior of an individual. They keep a person within the boundary of society and its culture. They provide us simple guidance as restrictions about something to do and something not to do. They guide our behavior and give us knowledge about wrong and right in our social reactions.

Social etiquettes help in building self esteem of a student. It falls under the essential responsibilities of parents to teach these social manners at the beginning of life itself. Any efforts now will pay off in the long run.

Address elders as "Sir" or "Ma'am"

Refer to females as ladies and males as gentlemen. Give respect and you will get respect.

Saying Thank you

When you get something or when someone helps you, say thanks. Also say "No thank you" when you do not want something.

Saying sorry

Everyone makes mistakes. Sometimes those mistakes can affect someone else. Like bumping into someone or running into someone. Say sorry, because it matters and it shows that you care.

Sharing

Sharing is the most admirable quality of a student. That shows his level of education. He may share with other children toys, books or eatables. It is a necessity for building friendship.

Table manners

Covering mouth when coughing stops germs from spreading . Speak only when the mouth is empty. Speak only after you have finished the mouthful so that you don't run the risk of covering the other person's body with food in your mouth. Similarly chew with mouth closed. Do not make noise while eating .Eat slowly and without making a noise .

Throw trash or garbage in a trash can

It is important that parents teach children to dispose of skins of fruits like bananas or wrappers of candies .Otherwise passersby may face serious accidents due to slip of legs when falling on them.

Address elders appropriately

Children must be taught to address older people with respect. This can be easily accomplished by teaching them salutations like uncle or aunty.

Speak without interrupting

Do not instinctively talk or interrupt while a man is already talking.

Ask for permission

Children should not take other people's things or to do something that is not part of their routine, without permission. This will particularly serve them well when they are in the homes of friends or in hostel.

Excuse Me

If you want people to turn to you, always say "excuse me".

Do not make a show of your negative emotions

It is okay to tell others and your parents when you are not feeling okay but making a public display of your foul mood is not right.

Do not make comments on other people's appearance

It is outright bad manners for anyone to comment on someone else's weight, height or skin color.

Say Good Morning

Always say Good morning to people you meet first time in the day.

Knock on doors that are shut before entering

Do not walk right into shut door. It's polite to knock and wait for a response

Try to enjoy your company and do not say 'I am bored' all the time

It's alright to sit idle sometimes and not shout over your lungs that you having nothing to do and hence you are bored.

Hold the door open for the person coming after you

Always ask if you can help

It's good to help others without disturbing your own task in hand.

Rule of Privacy

Your family's affairs are private and should be kept that way. It should not be discussed with outsiders.

Don't read others diary or letters.

Nobody will appreciate an invasion of his privacy. As a respect for the other individual's privacy we should not read their letters or diary.

Clean up

Leave the bathroom, toilet, and kitchen, bed room and TV room clean and tidy; don't leave your dirty dishes around the house.

Your wet towels or dirty dishes are your responsibility. If you share a room, then share the responsibility of keeping it clean and tidy

Telephone/mobile Etiquette

When placing a call, always state your name along with the name of the person you are calling.

Do not sound overly anxious, aggressive or pushy.

Do not carry on side conversations with other people around you while on telephone.

Always speak at a low tone so as not to disturb others.

Meeting and greeting guests

When friends or family members arrive a warm and friendly greeting is essential.

 Open the door and invite the guests in, smile and be welcoming

General Rules of Good Manners and Etiquette in Public Places:

Give up your seat for an adult, especially for an old person, a handicapped person or pregnant women.

Turn down your portable music; it is very irritating to hear that scratchy sound blasting continuously

Place your garbage in a bin.

While talking in a group ,keep your voice low.

Old people are easily intimidated, be kind, polite, respectful and helpful to them.

Open the door for others. In buildings or lifts allow senior persons to go through first while you hold the door open for them.

Be on time

No one likes to wait for others who are always late.

Personal space

Maintain personal space while talking to someone.

Learn to communicate:

Learn how to hold a decent conversation, with back-and-forth dialogue. Never monopolize a discussion. Never gossip about a person in his absence.

Use your cell phone sparingly in public.

It's never too late for an apology in relationship.

Always be sorry for your mistakes or even if you are in doubt. Sometimes it's better to bend than break. Relationships are very delicate and small issues can ruin it. So hold on to it tightly.

A handshake with the smile can beat even the best forms of greetings.

Do give credit whenever it due. Never forget to appreciate others for their good things.

Accept your Flaws

No one is perfect in this world. Try to accept your mistakes and correct them, instead of explaining and arguing on the same.

Thank Others

Always thank others for their help by any means.

Cooperate with parents, teachers and class-mates

You can help in using strategies to help you if you are open minded and share your experiences.

www.ingramcontent.com/pod-product-compliance
Lightning Source LLC
Chambersburg PA
CBHW051400280526
45784CB00007B/3031